All Scripture references taken from the KJV of the Holy Bible, unless otherwise indicated.

FAKE FRIENDS: *Prayers Against Betrayers*

by Dr. Marlene Miles

Freshwater Press 2025

Freshwaterpress9@gmail.com

ISBN: 978-1-967860-89-0

Paperback Version

Copyright 2025, Dr. Marlene Miles. All rights reserved. No part of this book may be reproduced, distributed, or transmitted by any means or in any means including photocopying, recording or other electronic or mechanical methods without prior written permission of the publisher except in the case of brief publications or critical reviews.

DEDICATION

To everyone who learned the hard way that closeness doesn't always mean loyalty. And to every heart that stayed soft even when people tried to harden it.

This book is dedicated to all who have grown up happy only to be shocked as an adult to find out that your favorite relative is competing with you – always has been, and really can't stand your guts.

You deserve healing, clarity, protection, and peace: This book is for you.

Author's Note

This book came to me unexpectedly. I didn't plan to write on betrayal, but life has a way of exposing themes that too many people carry quietly.

If you've ever been hurt by someone you trusted, these pages were written with you in mind. My hope is that you reclaim your power, recover your joy, and rediscover the strength God placed inside you
long before anyone misused it.

Thank you for allowing these prayers to meet you
in such personal places.

---

*Some people look like friends until
loyalty costs them something.*

Table of Contents

Author's Note 3

SECTION 1 — FORMER FRIENDS, FAKE FRIENDS & BEST FRIEND BETRAYALS 13

Heal Me From the Friend Who Turned Into a Stranger 14

Remove Fake Friends Who Smile but Resent Me 15

I Can't Believe They Told What I Shared in Confidence 16

Healing From the Friend Who Stole My Work 16

SECTION 2 — FAKE DATERS, GASLIGHTERS & LOVE BOMBERS .. 17

Deliver Me From the Ones Who Pretend to Love Me 18

Expose the Gaslighters Who Twist My Reality 19

Protect Me From Love Bombers 20

Deliver Me From the Ex Who Weaponized Our History 21

Don't Let Me Chase After People Who Don't Choose Me 22

Restore My Trust After Being Betrayed by Someone I Loved 23

SECTION 3 — Seasonal Friends, & Emotional Drainers 24

Help Me Understand the Friends Who Only Come for Refills 25

Protection from Emotional Drainers 26

Vacation & *Event* Friends Who Disappear 27

Friends of Convenience 28

SECTION 4 — PERSONALITY COPIERS & IDENTITY EXCHANGERS 29

Trying to Live My Life Instead of Their Own 31

Strength Against Personality Copiers 33

Copycats Who Imitate Me but Won't Acknowledge Me 34

Let Me Not Be Bothered by People Who Copy My Personality 36

People Who Try to Copy My Identity Online 38

People Who Try to Exchange Places with Me 39

SECTION 5 — WORKPLACE BETRAYALS & CORPORATE (and school) ACTORS 40

The One Who Stole My Work, Idea, or Creation 41

Corporate Actors 42

Lord, Expose Users Who Don't Credit 43

The Friend Who Stole What Was Meant for Me 44

SECTION 6 — PERFORMER-SAINTS & CHURCH HYPOCRISY 47

Lord, Hold My Hands When My Heart Is Hot... 48

Those Who Pretend to Be Holy 49

Wounds Caused in Your House 51

Protect Me From Performer-Saints 52

Lord, Help Me Respond With Grace, Not Reaction 53

Lord, Deliver Me From the Damage Done 54

Lord, Help Me Respond with Grace, Not Reaction 55

Remove the Emotional Bruises & Hurts 56

Move Me When (If) It's Time to Move 57

Don't Let Me Stay Where I No Longer Belong 58

SECTION 7 — TRANSITIONS, MOVEMENT & OUTGROWING ENVIRONMENTS 60

When I've Outgrown a Place 61

SECTION 8 – When Relatives are Your Betrayers 62

For The Hidden Jealousy Wound ... 69

For Healing from Hidden Jealousy in Close Family Members 72

Hidden Jealousy Sibs, Step-Sibs, Blended Sibs 73

For Relatives Who Pretended to Like Me 74

For the Sibling, Cousin Relative, Childhood Playmate Who Was Nice Around Adults but Cruel in Private 75

Breaking the Spirit of Competition in the Bloodline 76

Healing from Being the Target of Family Insecurity 77

Prayer Against Fake Honor and Counterfeit Kindness.................... 78

Healing from Betrayal Disguised as Friendship 78

Healing Childhood "Blind Spots" .. 79

Healing the Shock of Hidden Hatred 79

Healing from Relatives Who Secretly Wanted Me to Fail 80

Healing from Being Quietly Measured Behind My Back 81

Breaking the Impact of Adults Who Compared Me to Other Kids 82

Healing from Subtle Sabotage 82

Breaking Attachments to Family "Villains" 83

Healing from the Weapon of Silence 83

Healing from Being the Mirror for Others' Insecurities 84

Breaking the Impact of Favoritism 84

Healing from the One Who Copied You Out of Jealousy......................... 85

Healing from Lifelong Misunderstanding 85

Breaking the Fear of Family Gatherings..................................... 86

Breaking Shame Caused by Relatives 86

Healing from Being Mocked for My Personality or Gifts 87

Deliverance from Family Gossip Circles.. 87

Healing from Relatives Who Watched Me Suffer 88

Healing from Secret Family Rivals 88

Healing from Two-Faced Siblings, Cousins, Relatives and Friends..... 89

Healing from Childhood Betrayals 89

Healing from Being "The Light" in a Jealous Family............................. 90

Healing from Relatives Who Took Advantage of My Kindness 90

Restoring Confidence After Learning the Truth About Family 91

Lord, Make Sure It's Not Me 92

CLOSING PRAYER 1 95

Healing, Release & Restoration 96

Lord, Finish the Healing Work You Started in Me 97

Lord, Help Me Forgive Them All So I Can Be More Like You 98

FINAL DECREES— For Healing, Confidence & New Connections .. 102

Dear Reader 103

Prayer Books by this Author 104

FAKE FRIENDS

SECTION 1 — FORMER FRIENDS, FAKE FRIENDS & BEST FRIEND BETRAYALS

Some friendships end quietly.
Some betrayals come softly.
Some people were close until loyalty cost them something.

This section is for the ones who smiled with you, prayed with you, laughed with you —
and then wounded you in ways you didn't expect.

Heal Me From the Friend Who Turned Into a Stranger

Lord,
Heal me from the friend who slowly faded out,
who stopped choosing me,
who stopped showing up,
and left without explanation.

Strengthen me to release what no longer grows.
Help me stop rehearsing what happened.
Heal the space their absence created
and fill it with peace.

In the Name of Jesus, Amen.

Remove Fake Friends Who Smile but Resent Me

Father,
Expose the friends who pretend well
but celebrate my struggles,
envy my blessings,
and speak against me in secret.

Remove them gently,
peacefully,
and permanently.

Surround me with people who love me for real.

In the Name of Jesus, Amen.

I Can't Believe They Told What I Shared in Confidence

Lord, I trusted them with my truth
and they turned it into a story for others.

Heal the embarrassment,
the shock, and the betrayal.

Teach me to trust wisely.
Protect me from people who use my vulnerability
as their entertainment. In Jesus' Name. Amen.

Healing From the Friend Who Stole My Work

Father, You saw what they took —
my work, my idea, my song, my project.

Restore my confidence.
Restore my reputation. Restore my peace.

What was meant for me will return to me
in a way no one can steal again.

In Jesus' Name, Amen.

SECTION 2 — FAKE DATERS, GASLIGHTERS & LOVE BOMBERS

Some people don't date you — they perform for you.
They mimic love, rush intimacy, flood you with attention,
and then disappear or turn cold.

This section is for romantic betrayal that wasn't romance at all — just manipulation wrapped in affection.

Some people don't want love — they want access.

Deliver Me From the Ones Who Pretend to Love Me

Lord,
Protect me from people who act like partners
but think like users.

They showed attention,
spoke sweetness,
created connection—
but never intended to stay.

Cut the emotional ties.
Lift the confusion.
Break the attachment.

Help me release people
who pretended to care
just long enough to get what they wanted.

In the Name of Jesus, Amen.

---

*Love doesn't always end with honesty,
but healing always starts with truth.*

Expose the Gaslighters Who Twist My Reality

Father,
Expose anyone who lies so well
they make me question myself.

Silence their manipulation.
Break their influence.
Block their access.

Restore my clarity.
Reset my confidence.
Help me trust my intuition again.

Every twist, every distortion, every mental game—
cancel it now.

In Jesus' Name, Amen.

Protect Me From Love Bombers

Lord,
Help me see through the ones
who rush affection,
force intensity,
and mimic soul ties
only to abandon them later.

Give me Wisdom to separate
real love from emotional performance.

Block relationships rooted in
manipulation,
control,
or inconsistency.

Help me stop confusing attention
with intention.

In Jesus, Name. Amen.

Deliver Me From the Ex Who Weaponized Our History

Father,
I bring You the pain
of being hurt by someone
who once held my heart.

Deliver me from the memories they twisted,
the secrets they shared,
the stories they exaggerated,
the lies they told, and the bitterness they spread after the breakup.

Remove any shame I feel
for trusting them during the time
when they were worthy of that trust.
Remove the emotional residue
of conversations that still sting.
Remove the heaviness they left behind
when they walked away messy
instead of honest.

Lord, help me reclaim my power
from someone who didn't deserve it.

In the Name of Jesus, Amen.

Don't Let Me Chase After People Who Don't Choose Me

Father God,
Help me release the desire
to fix friendships that broke themselves.

Help me stop trying to prove my worth
to people who only valued me selectively.
Help me walk away gracefully
when someone shows me
I am not a priority.

Teach me that loyalty
is not proven by clinging to people —
but by clinging to You.

And fill the empty spaces
with peace, purpose,
and new connections
that mirror the love You give.

In Jesus' Name, Amen.

Restore My Trust After Being Betrayed by Someone I Loved

Lord,
Whether it was a friend,
a fake friend,
or an ex with access to my deepest places
— betrayal leaves scars.

I ask You to restore my trust
without restoring the relationship.
Restore, instead, my hope
without reopening old wounds.
Restore my confidence
without letting their actions define me.

Heal the part of me
that fears trusting again.
Heal the part that questions my judgment.
Heal the part that aches
from giving my heart to someone
who didn't know how to honor it.

Lord, let this hurt become my growth —
not my identity. In Jesus' Name, Amen.

SECTION 3 — Seasonal Friends, & Emotional Drainers

Some people aren't permanent —
they're seasonal, or situational.

They show up when they're empty,
when they're lonely,
or when they need your energy,
your ideas,
your personality,
your plans,
or your presence.

But once they feel full again,
they fade.

This section is for the ones who came
close for a moment,
copied what they needed,
and disappeared when the season
changed.

Help Me Understand the Friends Who Only Come for Refills

Lord,
Help me release the friends
who return only when they're drained.

They come for my company,
my encouragement,
my ideas,
my energy—
and disappear when they're full again.

Give me Peace in recognizing
that not everyone is meant to stay.

Protect my heart
from people who visit me emotionally
but never invest in me relationally.

In the Name of Jesus, Amen.

Protection from Emotional Drainers

Father,
Guard me from people
who pull and pull, they draw and draw,
but never pour back.

Help me set boundaries
without guilt.
Help me say "no"
without fear.

Refill what others drained.
Restore what constant giving has emptied.

Send people who pour into me
as much as I pour into them.

In the Name of Jesus, Amen.

Vacation & *Event* Friends Who Disappear

Lord,
Heal the disappointment
of new people who bonded with me
but only for a moment.

They followed my itinerary,
my plans,
my energy. They photobombed all my
vacation pix because we were suddenly
best friends—
and then vanished after the trip, after the
holiday, so that even today I ask, *"Who
were those people?"*.

Help me enjoy temporary people
without them invading my life, my event,
seminar, conference, or vacation and
without expecting permanent loyalty.

Teach me to hold lightly
what was never meant to last.

I disconnect myself, my soul, my spirit
and my expectations from them and wish
them well.

In the Name of Jesus, Amen.

"Friends" of Convenience

Lord,
Remove the ones who reach for me
only when it benefits them.

If I'm just their backup plan,
their comfort zone,
their entertainment, the one they think of
at the last minute, as the last result, the
ones who esteem me lightly as
their temporary confidence—
show me clearly.

You said in Your Word that whoever
esteems You lightly, You shall also
esteem lightly. Let me be like You, Lord
and not put too much emphasis on what
should not have emphasis.

Help me choose relationships
built on truth,
not convenience.

In the Name of Jesus, Amen.

SECTION 4 — PERSONALITY COPIERS & IDENTITY EXCHANGERS

Some people don't want to be your friend —
they want to be **you.**

They study your personality,
copy your style,
mirror your confidence,
repeat your phrases,
and imitate your ideas
as if your identity is something they can slip into.

They attach themselves quietly,
not for relationship,
but for absorption.
They gather your essence,
your presence,
your creativity,
even your online identity—
without ever recognizing the source they copied.

These are the *copiers*,
the *imitators*,
the *inspiration thieves*,
and the *exchangers*—
the ones who try to trade places with you
spiritually, emotionally, or socially.

Their imitation can feel
unnerving,
irritating,
even violating.
But imitation is not replacement.
Copying is not calling.
And no one can exchange themselves
into a destiny
that God wrote in your name.

This section is for the moments when you whisper:

"Lord… help me not to notice,
help me not to care,
and help me stay grounded in who I am."

Because the peace you carry
is worth more than the attention your
imitators crave.

**When imitators become limitators, it's
time to move on.**

Trying to Live My Life Instead of Their Own

Lord,
You see when someone doesn't just copy
small things, but tries to imitate my
whole life.

The relationships I build, the family I
create, the milestones I experience,
even the names I choose for my children.

You see when someone shadows my
steps year after year,
season after season,
as if my path is the blueprint
for their identity.

Lord, protect me from people
who copy out of envy, insecurity, or
obsession.
People who watch every move
just to repeat it.
People who mirror my blessings
but never honor the battles I fought to get
them.

Father, cover my children,
my future, my relationships,
and my legacy

from anyone who tries to attach
themselves to my destiny.

Break the spiritual and emotional
pressure of being silently imitated.
Lift the discomfort that comes
when someone tries to live a life
that isn't theirs to live.

Remind me that:
my story is mine,
my blessings are mine,
my children's purpose is theirs,
and nobody can duplicate
what You uniquely designed for us.

Lord, put up a wall of protection between
me and others, my kids and others who
should not have access to our lives on a
spiritual level.

Guard me from comparison. Guard me
from resentment. Guard me from the
heaviness of being copied so deeply.

And Lord…restore anything my family
lost from being overshadowed
by someone else's imitation.

Give us peace, protection,
confidence, and a future that cannot be
copied. In the Name of Jesus, Amen.

Strength Against Personality Copiers

Lord,
Protect me from people
who attach themselves to me
only to imitate me.

They borrow my style,
my voice,
my ideas,
my energy—
but never honor the source, which is You
by Your Holy Spirit.

Help me stay confident
in who You made me,
so no imitation can diminish
my originality.

In the Name of Jesus, Amen.

---

*Some people come for the moment—
not the journey.*

Copycats Who Imitate Me but Won't Acknowledge Me

Lord,
You see the people
who study me from a distance,
copy my style,
mirror my choices,
and imitate my creativity—
but never speak,
never honor,
never acknowledge
where they got it from.

They take my hairstyles,
my clothes,
my ideas,
my energy,
my uniqueness—
and wear it like it was theirs all along.

Father, guard my spirit
from the irritation that comes
when someone copies me
but refuses to connect with me.

Heal the sting of being imitated
by people who won't even say hello.
Heal the frustration of watching my originality
become someone else's identity.

Remind me that imitation
is proof of the gift You placed inside me—
not a threat to it.

Protect my confidence.
Protect my creativity.
Protect my individuality.

Let my style, my ideas, and my presence
keep evolving faster
than anyone can copy.

And Lord, help me stay gracious
even when the copying is obvious…
because nobody can outshine
the original You created.

In the Name of Jesus, Amen.

Let Me Not Be Bothered by People Who Copy My Personality
...unless it is affecting destiny

Lord,
Some people don't just copy my style
they copy me.

My expressions, my mannerisms,
my humor, my energy, my way of
moving through the world.

But Father... help me not notice so much.
Help me not care. Help me rise above the
irritation when someone imitates my
personality instead of developing their
own.

Protect my identity. Protect my
originality. Protect my inner world
from those who try to wear it
like a costume. And remind me that
what You placed in me cannot be
duplicated— only imitated. In the Name
of Jesus, Amen.

***Some friends were never friends
just good actors in the right season.***

People Who Try to Copy My Identity Online

Lord,
You see anyone who steals my pictures,
mimics my voice,
copies my content,
or tries to imitate my presence online
as if my life is their blueprint.

Block their attempts.
Shut down their access.
Protect my digital identity
from anyone who wants to use it
for attention, deception, or imitation,
unless it is to bring glory to You.

And Lord… help me not to obsess,
overthink, or worry about it.
Remind me that nobody can steal
who I truly am as long as I am in You.

Guard my name, my likeness,
my ideas, and my online footprint. Help
me not to put all my private business
online. But, let the real me
always shine clearer than the imitation.

In Jesus' Name, Amen.

People Who Try to Exchange Places with Me

Lord, protect me from people who don't just copy— they try to exchange or replace.

People who want my role,
my relationships, my opportunities,
my position, or my influence.

People who attach themselves
to absorb my confidence, my identity, or
my *being*.

Lord, help me not fixate on them.
Help me not fear them. Help me not give them a second of emotional or spiritual power.

Guard my space. Guard my energy. Guard the assignments with my name on them. What You gave me cannot be exchanged, taken, stolen, or swapped by anyone pretending to be me.

Cover me, Lord, from every form of imitation— and keep me grounded in the original identity You created.

In the Name of Jesus, Amen.

SECTION 5 — WORKPLACE BETRAYALS & CORPORATE (and school) ACTORS

(Co-workers who pretend, compete, copy, or steal credit)

Some co-workers wear badges —
others wear masks.

This section is for the ones who
act friendly but move jealous,
who praise you publicly
but sabotage you quietly,
and who steal your ideas
while pretending they support you.

The One Who Stole My Work, Idea, or Creation

Lord,
You saw what they took —
my project, my idea, my song, my
concept, my effort.

Heal the sting of seeing someone else
receive glory for what I labored over.

Restore my confidence.
Restore my creativity.
Restore my peace.

Elevate me so clearly
that no one can mistake
who You have truly gifted.

In the Name of Jesus, Amen.

Corporate Actors

Father,
Shield me from co-workers
who smile in meetings
but scheme in private.

Block their jealousy.
Expose their motives.
Confuse their plans.

Surround me with people
who want collaboration—
not competition disguised as friendship.

In the Name of Jesus, Amen.

Lord, Expose Users Who Don't Credit

Lord, reveal peers and leaders
who take my work
but hide my name.

Expose the ones
who ask for my ideas
but present them as their own.

Give me Wisdom
to know when to help
and when to step back.

Reward me openly
for what was taken secretly. In the Name
of Jesus, Amen.

The Friend Who Stole What Was Meant for Me

Lord,
Some betrayals come quietly,
but this one came like a strike to the heart.

A person I loved,
a friend I trusted,
used our bond as a shortcut
to take what was meant for me.

They took the credit that belonged to my work.
They stepped into the role I earned.
They claimed the honor I was chosen for.
They accepted the opportunity shaped in my name.
Or they pursued someone I cared for
while pretending to care about me.

God, I never expected to be hurt
by someone who knew my dreams,
my insecurities,
my journey,
and my heart.
But they used that knowledge
as leverage.

Lord, heal the sting of watching someone
take a blessing that I labored for,
prayed for,
prepared for,
and waited for.

Heal the humiliation
of being blindsided
by someone who I once called "friend."

Heal the anger that rises
when I remember how they smiled in my face
while planning behind my back.

And Father, deliver me
from believing that what they took
was truly mine.

If it WAS meant for me, Lord, make sure
they can't keep it.
And if it wasn't,
give me the Wisdom
to let it go
and trust the path You preserved for my life.

Elevate me beyond what was stolen.
Promote me beyond what was taken.
Honor me in ways that silence the lie
that they won anything by their betrayal.

Lord, restore my Peace,
restore my confidence,
and restore my sense of worth
after being betrayed by someone
who knew exactly how much they were hurting me
and did it anyway.

In Jesus' Name, Amen.

Not everyone at the table came to work — some came to watch, copy, and compete. Some came to eat where they prepared nothing.

Lord, if you didn't say feed them, let them not take from me. In Jesus' Name.

SECTION 6 — PERFORMER-SAINTS & CHURCH HYPOCRISY

Believers Until the Pastor Walks Away

Some people act holy when eyes are on them
and switch spirits when no one is watching.

This section is for church hurt, sanctuary actors,
leadership politics,
favoritism,
and spiritual hypocrisy that wounds deeply.

Lord, Hold My Hands When My Heart Is Hot

Lord,
When church people poke my patience,
steady me.
When their words sting,
calm me.
When I want to respond in anger,
cover me.

Help me stay grounded
even when others act up.
Give me Peace that reacts slower
than my frustration.

In the Name of Jesus, Amen.

Those Who Pretend to Be Holy

Lord,
Some people put on holiness like a
costume—whether in leadership or on the
pew beside me.
They perform righteousness
but practice deception.
They act saved
but move like saboteurs.
They pretend to love You
but mistreat Your people when no one is
looking.

Father, protect me from these hidden
enemies.
Expose their motives,
confuse their schemes,
silence their gossip,
and block their attempts to harm my
Peace.

Cover me with Your favor
when their jealousy rises.
Cover me with Your Truth
when their lies circulate.
Cover me with Your love
when their behavior tries to steal my joy.

And Lord, protect my heart.
Don't let their actions harden me.
Don't let their hypocrisy make me cynical.
Don't let their darkness dim my light.

Keep me spiritually sharp
and emotionally grounded.
Let me walk in discernment
and stand in Wisdom.

In Jesus' Name, Amen.

Wounds Caused in Your House

Father,
Church wounds cut deeply because they
land in places meant for healing.
They bruise the trust placed in
community,
and weaken the hope I had in fellowship.

I bring You the pain caused by the ones
who sing songs of salvation
but speak words that tear down.

Lord, stitch up the places in me that were
ripped open. Repair my Peace.
Restore my confidence.
Rebuild my ability to love past
disappointment.

Heal the private places where I've cried
alone
after being hurt by people who should
have known better.

In the Name of Jesus, Amen.

Protect Me From Performer-Saints

God,
Some people wear salvation like a costume. They rehearse kindness, perform humility, and act righteous only when someone important is watching.

But when the pastor steps away,
their real character walks forward.

Lord, cover me.
Protect me from their schemes.
Shield me from their jealousy,
their gossip, their bitterness, and their quiet attempts to undermine me.

Let no false believer drain my spirit.
Let no imitation saint sabotage my purpose.
Let no undercover enemy interrupt the work You are doing in me.

Surround me with truth,
discernment, and divine protection.

In Jesus' Name, Amen.

Lord, Help Me Respond With Grace, Not Reaction

Father,
You know the temptation:
to clap back, snap back,
or match the energy given to me.

But Lord, I am asking You to elevate my reactions.
Help me speak wisely, not angrily.
Help me pause instead of explode.
Help me breathe instead of break.

When I feel provoked,
let Your peace rise faster than my irritation.
When I feel attacked,
let Your presence defend me better than my words could.

Lord, give me the maturity
to respond like someone who belongs to You
and not like someone controlled by the moment. In the Name of Jesus, Amen.

Lord, Deliver Me From the Damage Done

God,
I am not just asking for protection from people —
I am asking for deliverance from the **after-effects** of their behavior.

Deliver me from the overthinking,
the embarrassment,
the replaying of conversations,
the emotional bruises that linger.

Deliver me from the insecurity planted by their actions,
and from the fear of trusting again.

Heal my mind from the negativity they stirred.
Heal my heart from the wounds they caused.
Heal my spirit from the heaviness they left behind.

Lord, undo the damage —
Make me whole again
from what people damaged
while pretending to serve You.

In the Name of Jesus, Amen.

Lord, Help Me Respond with Grace, Not Reaction

God,
Give me the strength
to respond with Wisdom
instead of emotion.

Let Peace rise faster
than irritation.
Let calm sit deeper
than offense.

Help me speak with maturity,
not anger.

In the Name of Jesus, Amen.

Remove the Emotional Bruises & Hurts

Lord,
Remove the emotional bruises
left by gossip,
favoritism,
lies,
and spiritual manipulation.

Lift the weight.
Break the fear.
Heal the places I carry quietly.

In the Name of Jesus, Amen.

Move Me When (If) It's Time to Move

Lord,
If this place is no longer feeding me,
show me.
If it's time to shift,
move me.
If You want me to stay,
settle me.

I follow Your direction,
not my frustration.

In the Name of Jesus, Amen.

Don't Let Me Stay Where I No Longer Belong

Father,
If I've outgrown this environment,
free me.
If the season is over,
close it.
If the Grace is gone,
lift me out.

Father, if I am in the wrong place because of a faulty spiritual foundation--, Lord, heal my foundation so I can live and function properly to the praise of Your Glory.

Show me the right place I should be.

Help me leave without guilt
and walk into places
that honor who I am becoming.

In the Name of Jesus, Amen.

---

*Some people worship loudly,
but live truth quietly.
Discernment is protection.*

Reflection —

When God Starts Making You Uncomfortable.

It is because He is showing you something you need to pray about, OR He may be nudging you that it is time to go.

When God wants to move you, He lets the comfort fade. He lets things feel tight, heavy, or draining.
It's not punishment —
it's preparation.

I move when God moves.

SECTION 7 — TRANSITIONS, MOVEMENT & OUTGROWING ENVIRONMENTS

Every place isn't forever.
Every season isn't lifelong.
Sometimes God grows you past people, circles, ministries, and environments.

This section is for moments when you feel spiritually tight, emotionally drained, or uncomfortable —
and you're not sure if it's time to move or time to stay.

My next season will fit me better than the last.

When I've Outgrown a Place

Lord,
Sometimes things feel tight
because I've grown.

Give me wisdom to recognize
when a season can't hold me anymore.

Lead me into bigger, healthier places
that match who You're shaping me to be.

I walk forward without fear—
because You lead the way.

In Jesus' Name, Amen.

REFLECTION —

*When God shifts you,
your spirit outgrows places long before
your body does.*

SECTION 8 – When Relatives are Your Betrayers

If there is anything worse than a fake friend it is a fake relative, a fake sibling, a fake cousin, aunt or uncle. Unfortunately, even parents can be fake. Now, don't be paranoid; be prayerful. Be discerning, be wise. Be your genuine self; be strong in the Lord.

This hits different because siblings, cousins-- relatives are supposed to be your first friends, your childhood safety, your play partners, your holiday memories, your "built-in family" So when you grow up cheerful, innocent, loving, thinking everything is fine, but later realize they were competing with you, resenting you, or quietly hating on you the whole time it can be quite a shock.

And a man's foes shall be they of his own household. (Matthew 10:36)

All kinds of people are born into the world every day; God loved Jacob and hated Esau and they were twins. If you believe you ae one of the "good" ones, don't let that go to your head. If God is showing you something it is because you have work to do; your job is to do something about it. We don't judge others – yes, their actions, we don't blame, we don't accuse, we pray and govern ourselves accordingly. Pray for them, unless God says otherwise. Jesus can save all of us.

That is, They which are the children of the flesh, these are not the children of God: but the children of the promise are counted for the seed. (Romans 9:8)

But as an adult you may look back and see that your childhood "friends" (or relatives) weren't friends at all, but maybe adversaries. Well, it feels like betrayal, confusion, shock, grief, and a strange kind of emotional whiplash. It shakes your sense of memory. It shatters the way you thought your childhood was. And it leaves you questioning: *"Was I imagining everything? Was I blind? Why didn't I see it?"*

Don't gird up for war, gird up for discernment and prayer.

That reaction is NORMAL. Because **you were a child.** You weren't supposed to detect jealousy. You weren't supposed to decode hidden animosity. The average kid just knows that a person is either nice or mean. And whatever kind of playdate you had today, you'd forgive it, forget it and be back on the playground tomorrow. You weren't supposed to or equipped to analyze behavior. And you certainly weren't supposed to protect yourself from "family."

Now, that's your brother (sister, cousin, friend), go say you're sorry. This is what the grown folks told you, so you did it.

And, since the grown folks were running this, you were pretty much assured that you were SAFE.

And you were being yourself — open-hearted, joyful, pure, loving — because that's who you ARE. Their conflict wasn't about you. It was about their insecurity, their upbringing, their wounds, their comparisons from adults, the attention you got, the favor or personality you carried, the Grace God put on your life.

People—, especially children, react to those things from a place of brokenness.

Here's the painful truth: Some relatives resent what they sense on your life — even when you are too young to understand what's happening spiritually. And many cousins grow up competing with someone who wasn't competing with them at all.

Your shock is the shock of innocence discovering hidden hostility. There is a grief in that. A deep one.

But here is the good news: You can heal. You can reclaim your childhood memories. You can break the spiritual residue of their jealousy.

You can bless them without binding yourself to their wounds. And you can walk away stronger, wiser, and clean-hearted — without carrying the weight of their issues anymore.

Lord, heal me from the shock of discovering hidden hatred in my family, in the Name of Jesus.

This shock brings the wound of the "smiling enemy." The one who acted nice, laughed with you, hugged you at holidays, posed in pictures, smiled in your face, seemed "fine" for decades, but internally **held jealousy, competition, or resentment**

And you never knew. You didn't see it. You didn't suspect it. Because you're not wired like that. You grew up happy. You grew up open-hearted. You grew up loving them genuinely. You thought the relationship was real.

And then, **adult revelation hits**: *"She never liked me." "She was* *competing with me." "She couldn't stand me." "She was hiding it the whole time."* That kind of discovery shakes your spirit because it forces you to reevaluate your memories, your relationship, your innocence, your trust, your discernment, your ability to "read people," the truth of your childhood experiences. And that's not small. That's a **soul-level heartbreak.**

The older sibling of a mean cousin, for example, often plays the role of the "responsible one," the "nice one," the "balanced one," the "mature one." The older one is the one who is watching out for you and you most often yielded leadership into their hands. They were protecting you when the grown folks weren't around. So, you naturally expected warmth or safety from her. But here's what you need to know (and this will set you free):

Some of the worst jealousy is the jealousy that hides quietly. Jealousy that behaves. Jealousy that smiles. Jealousy that pretends. Jealousy that plays polite.

Jealousy that waits until adulthood to reveal its true colors. Jealousy that wasn't dealt with while you grew up — so it calcified.

Sometimes the older sister wasn't "mean as cuss," not because she wasn't jealous but because she learned how to disguise it better.

Children show their jealousy through cruelty. Older children show it through **silence, comparison, and hidden competition.**

Adults show it through **distance, coldness, hostility, or subtle disrespect.** Jealousy matures — but it doesn't disappear. The MEAN cousin was the obvious wound. But the older sister was the **covert wound** the one that blindsided you in adulthood because she masked it.

That betrayal goes deep.
But God heals even this.

For The Hidden Jealousy Wound

(The sibling, step-sibling, cousin, relative, fake friend who secretly resented you.)

Lord, I bring before You the sibling, the cousin, the relative or the fake friend who acted kind,
but secretly resented me.
The one who smiled, but competed.
Who embraced me, but envied me.
Who stayed polite, but never loved me.
Who hid her jealousy behind maturity, calmness, silence, and fakery.

Heal me from the shock of discovering the truth later in life.
Heal the grief of realizing the closeness I felt wasn't mutual.
Heal the confusion that comes from hidden hostility.
Heal the pain of being blindsided by family betrayal.

Lord, remove every lie I believed because I was innocent.
Remove the sting of broken trust.
Restore my ability to discern without fear. Restore my confidence in my own purity and goodness.

I break the power of every silent jealousy, every unspoken curse, every silent comparison, every hidden rivalry directed toward me.

I release her (him). I forgive her (him). But I reclaim my spirit from her (their) influence. I reclaim my memories from her (their) resentment.
I reclaim my self-worth from their silent hatred.

Lord, lift this burden from my heart and seal my healing with Your Peace.
In Jesus' Name—Amen.

Marvel not if they hate you; they hated Me first. Love, Jesus.

If the world hate you, ye know that it hated me before it hated you. (John 15:18)

ADVANCED PRAYERS FOR DEEPER HEALING

Family doesn't always behave like family. Sometimes the closest titles hold the deepest wounds.

For Healing from Hidden Jealousy in Close Family Members

Lord, heal the wounds caused by family members who secretly envied me.
Those who smiled but resented,
who hugged but competed,
who congratulated but inwardly wished against me.

I break the power of hidden jealousy.
I release myself from its shadow.
I am free from envy, and free from being envied.
In Jesus' Name. Amen.

Hidden Jealousy Sibs, Step-Sibs, Blended Sibs

Lord, heal my very soul from the wounds caused by step-sibs, blended family, blended households, foster sibs, or polygamous households where I was forced to get along with kids or others or they were forced to get along with me.

Heal the effects of secret envy, hidden ill intents, concealed jealousy, competition, gossip, fibbing, and backbiting.

Those who smiled but resented,
who hugged but competed,
who may have congratulated openly, but inwardly competed, hated and wished against me.

I break the power of hidden jealousy.
I release myself from its shadow.
I am free from envy, and free from being envied. Lord heal all of us from having to share parents who didn't have enough to give, In Jesus' Name. Amen.

For Relatives Who Pretended to Like Me

Lord, heal the betrayal of relatives who pretended to love me,
acted friendly,
but held bitterness or contempt in private.

Especially the interrogators—those who just made conversation to find out what you were doing or what you were up to so they could compete or derail your plans.

Restore my trust.
Cleanse my heart of confusion.
Seal my spirit from false love.
In the Name of Jesus, Amen.

For the Sibling, Cousin Relative, Childhood Playmate Who Was Nice Around Adults but Cruel in Private

Lord, heal me from the cousin who hid their cruelty behind manners.
The one who performed kindness for adults,
but wounded me when no one saw.

Break the power of that two-faced, double-faced behavior.
Restore my sense of safety.
Heal every hidden bruise on my heart.

And now that I am older, let me not offend or disrespect any parent, adult or elder as I choose how to continue or discontinue my relationship with those who constantly hurt me in childhood and never truly apologized.

In the Name of Jesus, Amen.

Breaking the Spirit of Competition in the Bloodline

Lord, I break the generational *spirit of competition*.
Competition for love.
Competition for attention.
Competition for approval.
Competition for position.
Competition for validation.

I do not choose that family members are opponents. But I will walk in Love using Wisdom and discernment.

Lord, break the spirit of competition or money and toys and gifts from parents so that we have more than another.

Break that spirit in our bloodline, in the Name of Jesus.

Father, it is beautiful when we can all dwell together in unity. Unite us in purpose, not rivalry.
In the Name of Jesus, Amen.

Healing from Being the Target of Family Insecurity

Lord, heal me from the wounds caused by feeling unsafe or insecure growing up.

Lord, heal me from the wounds caused by insecure relatives—
those who attacked me because they felt inferior,
those who compared themselves to me,
those who punished me for gifts You gave, or just because I exist.

Let me shrink no more, but let me be all You have designed and called me to be.

Lift their insecurity off my identity.
In the Name of Jesus, Amen.

Prayer Against Fake Honor and Counterfeit Kindness

Lord, expose and break the influence of
false kindness and feigned interest from
those who pretended to honor me,
yet carried resentment in their hearts.

Deliver me from counterfeit affection.
Let only sincere love take root in my life.
In Jesus' Name, Amen.

Healing from Betrayal Disguised as Friendship

Lord, heal the wound of cousins or
siblings who acted like friends,
but betrayed me behind my back.

Remove the sting.
Restore my sense of trust.
Redeem my memories.
In Jesus' Name, Amen.

Healing Childhood "Blind Spots"

Lord, heal every wound I could not interpret as a child— moments I didn't understand, behaviors I couldn't explain, hostility I couldn't decode.

Restore clarity. Restore peace.
Restore innocence.
In Jesus' Name, Amen.

Healing the Shock of Hidden Hatred

Lord, heal the shock of discovering, later in life, that a relative I loved could not stand me.

Minister to the grief of that revelation. Heal the part of me that feels foolish, blindsided, or hurt. Replace shock with peace. In Jesus' Name, Amen.

Healing from Relatives Who Secretly Wanted Me to Fail

Lord, heal me from the relatives who
hoped I wouldn't succeed—
who resented my progress,
who downplayed my joy,
who silently envied every blessing.

Break their silent wishes off my destiny.
In Jesus' Name, Amen.

Healing from Being Quietly Measured Behind My Back

Lord, break the power of comparisons
made behind closed doors—
every whispered assessment of my life,
every critique spoken in secret,
every evaluation based on jealousy.

I refuse to be measured by wounded people.
You define me, Lord.
In the Name of Jesus, Amen.

Breaking the Impact of Adults Who Compared Me to Other Kids

Lord, break the words spoken by adults
who compared me to other children—
that shaped my worth,
shaped my confidence,
shaped my perception of myself.

I renounce those comparisons.
Restore my identity.
In the Name of Jesus, Amen.

Healing from Subtle Sabotage

Lord, heal every wound from relatives
who subtly undermined me—
those who discouraged my dreams,
downplayed my strengths,
or tried to block my opportunities.

Remove their influence from my path.
In Jesus' Name, Amen.

Breaking Attachments to Family "Villains"

Lord, break emotional attachments to relatives who hurt me deeply.
Those who traumatized, manipulated, or intimidated. Break every soul tie with them and unpleasant memories.
I release them.
I detach from their influence.
I reclaim my peace.
In Jesus' Name, Amen.

Healing from the Weapon of Silence

Lord, heal me from relatives who punished me with silence—
the cold shoulder, the quiet disdain, the passive-aggressive withdrawal.

Break the power of silent rejection.
In Jesus' Name, Amen.

Healing from Being the Mirror for Others' Insecurities

Lord, heal me from being the sibling or cousin who reflected
others' insecurities back to them—
the one they projected onto,
envied, resented,
or competed against.

I am not responsible for their wounds.
In Jesus' Name, Amen.

Breaking the Impact of Favoritism

Lord, break the wounds caused by favoritism I didn't recognize as a child—
the subtle cues,
the quiet biases,
the invisible hierarchies.

Heal me from their emotional imprint.
In Jesus' Name, Amen.

Healing from the One Who Copied You Out of Jealousy

Lord, heal the frustration and resentment from being copied— when relatives mocked me or mimicked my style, my personality, my gifts, or my identity.

Restore my uniqueness.
Restore my freedom to shine.
In Jesus' Name, Amen.

Healing from Lifelong Misunderstanding

Lord, heal the pain of never being understood by my family—
of being misread,
misjudged,
misinterpreted.

Cover me with the comfort of being fully known by You. In Jesus' Name, Amen.

Breaking the Fear of Family Gatherings

Lord, break the anxiety tied to family gatherings— the dread, the discomfort, the memories of conflict or pain.

Replace fear with Wisdom, Peace, and boundaries. In Jesus' Name, Amen.

Breaking Shame Caused by Relatives

Lord, break every shameful memory caused by teasing, mocking, or humiliating relatives.

Lift shame off my identity.
I walk in dignity. In the Name of Jesus, Amen.

Healing from Being Mocked for My Personality or Gifts

Lord, heal me from relatives who made
fun of my voice, my body,
my dreams, my intelligence,
my joy,
my creativity,
my calling.

Restore what was mocked.
In the Name of Jesus, Amen.

Deliverance from Family Gossip Circles

Lord, break the power of relatives who
gossiped about me—
who spread stories,
misrepresented me,
or tarnished my name.

Restore my reputation in Heaven's
courts. In the Name of Jesus. Amen.

Healing from Relatives Who Watched Me Suffer

Lord, heal me from the pain of family members who stood by
while others mistreated me—
who saw the injustice
and said nothing.

Restore every unprotected part of me.
In the Name of Jesus. Amen.

Healing from Secret Family Rivals

Lord, heal me from relatives who saw me as competition—
who treated me as a threat,
not a blessing.

Break rivalry.
Break comparison.
Break covert hostility.
In Jesus' Name, Amen.

Healing from Two-Faced Siblings, Cousins, Relatives and Friends.

Lord, heal me from cousins who were sweet one moment and harsh the next—unpredictable, unstable, and emotionally unsafe. Break the confusion tied to their dual behavior.
In the Name of Jesus, Amen.

Healing from Childhood Betrayals

Lord, heal every betrayal of childhood—
secrets told,
trust broken,
confidence violated,
friendship misused.

Cleanse every scar left behind.
In the Name of Jesus, Amen.

Healing from Being "The Light" in a Jealous Family

Lord, heal the burden of being the bright one in a family that resented my light.

Break jealousy.
Break resentment.
Break silent hatred.
Let my light shine freely.
In Jesus' Name, Amen.

Healing from Relatives Who Took Advantage of My Kindness

Lord, heal the wound of being used—
taken for granted,
taken advantage of,
manipulated,
or exploited.

Restore my boundaries.
Restore my confidence.
In Jesus' Name. Amen.

Restoring Confidence After Learning the Truth About Family

Lord, restore my confidence after
discovering the truth—
after realizing who loved me,
who resented me,
who envied me,
and who never understood me.

Rebuild me.
Strengthen me.
Stabilize me.
And establish me in unshakeable identity.

In Jesus' Name—Amen.

Lord, Make Sure It's Not Me

Lord,
As I pray about the people who have hurt me, I also look inward.

If there is anything in me
that acts like the very things I fear —
change it.
Heal it. Remove it.

Lord, **make sure it's not me.**

Don't let me become a fake friend
who smiles up close
but resents in silence.

Don't let me be a user
who takes more than I give
or drains people dry.

Don't let me be a copier who imitates others instead of growing into my own identity.

Don't let me be an exchanger
who tries to take someone else's
blessings, opportunities,
or place in life.

Don't let me be a gaslighter
who twists truth or makes people
question themselves.

Don't let me be a stealer
of ideas, credit, attention, or peace.

Search my heart, Lord.
Clean my motives.
Purify my intentions.
Align my character with who You created
me to be.

Every time I've been wrong,
reveal it so I can make it right.
If I've ever hurt someone,
teach me to apologize and grow.
If I've ever behaved from insecurity,
heal the root so I never repeat it.

Lord…
protect me not only from fake friends —
but from becoming one.

Shape me.
Correct me.
Grow me.
Strengthen me.
And keep me real
in every relationship I have.

In the Name of Jesus, Amen.

Every betrayal leaves a mark, but every prayer lifts you closer to wholeness.

CLOSING PRAYER 1

Lord,
Thank You for walking with me
through every memory, every wound,
every betrayal,
and every moment that made me question
my strength.

Thank You for healing my heart
from the actions of people I once trusted.
Thank You for restoring my confidence
where it was shaken.
Thank You for lifting the weight of pain
that I carried silently for too long.

Going forward, surround me with real
friends, real supporters, real love, and
real connections that reflect Your heart
and not human weakness.

Protect me from hidden enemies.
Protect me from pretenders.
Protect me from those who want my light
but not my well-being.

And most of all, Lord, protect my spirit
so betrayal never changes who I am —
only who I choose to walk with.

In the Name of Jesus, Amen.

Healing, Release & Restoration

You're Rising from What Tried to Break You

Every betrayal taught you something:
who's real,
who's seasonal,
who's draining,
who's dangerous,
who's good for your soul,
and who was only pretending.

But most importantly,
it taught you something about *yourself*—
your resilience,
your discernment,
your strength,
and your capacity to heal.

You didn't lose anything real.
You lost illusions.
And now you rise with clarity.

Lord, Finish the Healing Work You Started in Me

Lord,
Thank You for walking me through every
wound, every disappointment,
every betrayal,
and every confusing connection.

Finish the healing in the places
that still feel tender.
Lift the heaviness that tries to linger.
Close every door that no longer serves
my future. Open every door
that leads to peace, truth, and real
connection.

Protect me from fake friends, fake lovers,
fake supporters,
and anyone who wears a mask around my
heart.

Surround me with real people
who bring safety, sincerity, and
reciprocity. And let betrayal never harden
me— only sharpen me.

In Jesus' Name, Amen.

Lord, Help Me Forgive Them All So I Can Be More Like You

Lord,
You see every wound I've carried
from fake friends,
jealous relatives,
seasonal connections,
copycats,
users,
gaslighters,
love bombers,
performer-saints,
and the people who smiled close
while moving against me in secret.

You see the cousins who acted like strangers,
the friends who acted like enemies,
the coworkers who stole what I created,
the relatives who betrayed trust,
the church folk who performed holiness,
and the people who entered my life
only to drain, imitate, or disappear.

Father… these hurts were real.
They cut deep.
They shocked me.
They disappointed me.
They shaped parts of my heart
I'm still trying to understand.

But today, Lord,
I choose **forgiveness** —
not because they were right,
not because they apologized,
not because they deserved it, but because
I offer Grace,
and because *I* deserve Peace,
and because forgiveness
makes me more like Jesus.

So Father, I release:

- the lies that were told about me
- the secrets shared in betrayal
- the love that was imitated, not given
- the work that was stolen
- the friendship that wasn't real
- the trust that was mishandled
- the jealousy that was hidden
- the manipulation that confused me

- the performances that hurt me
- the people who used my heart
- the people who copied my life
- the family who acted like strangers
- the strangers who acted too close
- and the ones who disappeared

as soon as their season was over.

Lord, I let it all go.
I place every offense
at Your feet.

I refuse to let bitterness
be my inheritance.
I refuse to let anger
shape my identity.
I refuse to let betrayal
block my blessings.

Make my heart lighter.
Make my spirit cleaner.
Make my mind clearer.
Make my life freer.

In forgiving them, Lord,
free **me**.
Heal me.
Lift me.

Grow me.
Transform me.

And help me become
a little more like Jesus —
merciful,
gracious,
unbothered,
and unburdened
by what people tried to take from me.

Thank You for the strength to forgive.
Thank You for the courage to release.
Thank You for the Peace that's coming next.

In the Name of Jesus, Amen.

      Always forgive, but remember forgiveness does not mean renewed access. Be sure you discern and hear from the Lord regarding who gets access to you, your life, your family, your career, your ministry and your life.

FINAL DECREES— For Healing, Confidence & New Connections

1. I leave every false friend behind me, in Jesus' Name.
2. My heart is protected, not guarded, in Jesus' Name.
3. I no longer apologize for requiring honesty, in Jesus' Name.
4. I move forward with clarity, not fear, in Jesus' Name.
5. I attract real love, real friends, real support, in Jesus' Name.
6. Betrayal did not break me — it built me, in Jesus' Name.
7. I walk into my next season whole, in Jesus' Name.
8. Only real ones can stay, in the Name of Jesus.

AMEN

Dear Reader

Thank you for acquiring, reading and praying with this prayer manual.

I pray the Lord has richly blessed you and if you are not suddenly delivered, may the Lord do His perfect work in you in His timing by His Grace and your own faith. Be healed. Be made whole. In Jesus' Name, Amen.

Shalom,

Dr. Marlene Miles

Prayer Books by this Author

Prayer Manuals

FAKE FRIENDS: *Prayers Against Betrayers*

HOLIDAY WARFARE Prayer Manual (humorous) Surviving Family Gatherings All Year Long (without catching a case)

SOUL TIE Prayer Manual (The) Part of a 3-part series including a workbook.

MAD at DADDY Prayer Manual – part of a 3-part series including a workbook.

Healing the Sibling & Relative Wound Prayer Manual

Healing the Father-Son Wound Prayer Manual

Prayers Against Barrenness: *For Success in Business and Life*

Breaking Curses of the Mother Prayer Manual

Fruit of the Womb: *Prayers Against Barrenness*

Beauty Curses, *Warfare Prayers Against*
https://a.co/d/5Xlc2OM

Courts of Marriage: Prayers for Marriage in the Courts of Heaven *(prayerbook)*
https://a.co/d/cNAdgAq

Courtroom Warfare @ Midnight *(prayerbook)* https://a.co/d/5fc7Qdp

Dr. Miles has written many more titles on relevant subjects, available on many platforms, especially amazon/kindle in digital, print and audio formats.

About the Author

Dr. Marlene Miles writes from a place of lived experience, personal healing, and a deep desire to see others whole. She knows what it feels like to carry painful words, to struggle with identity, and to long for God to rewrite the story. Through her journey, she discovered the power of prayer, reflection, and Scripture in transforming the heart.

Today, she shares those revelations with others—helping them break cycles, heal emotionally, and discover the beauty of God's truth over their lives. Her ministry flows with gentleness, honesty, and a prophetic sensitivity that reaches hearts right where they are.

Her calling is to help the broken become whole, the weary find rest, and the wounded step into purpose. Every book she writes is an offering of healing, hope, and freedom.

www.ingramcontent.com/pod-product-compliance
Lightning Source LLC
Chambersburg PA
CBHW070853050426
42453CB00012B/2182